The Department of Work and Pensions Assesses a Jade Fish

First published in 2024 by Blue Diode Press
30 Lochend Road
Leith
Edinburgh EH6 8BS
www.bluediode.co.uk

ISBN: 978-1-915108-17-3

Typesetting: Rob A. Mackenzie and Amy Curtis
text in Pilgrim LT Roman

Front cover art: fishing hooks, by Sveta, Adobe Stock.
jade fish, public domain
Back cover art: 'Child Riding on Walking Frame'
by Isabelle & Irene McIver
Cover design and typography: Rob A. Mackenzie & Amy Curtis

Diode logo design: Sam and Ian Alexander

Printed and bound by Imprint Digital, Exeter, UK.
https://digital.imprint.co.uk

The Department of Work and Pensions Assesses a Jade Fish

NUALA WATT

BLUE DIODE PRESS

For Isabelle

in memoriam
Catherine Mary Walker
11th February 1962–23rd July 2017

in memoriam
Sheila Templeton
17 August 1941–26th November 2023

CONTENTS

Receiving My Poems in Braille

My thoughts have arrived in the post.
I don't know which ones.
I think they may be cyclists in the dark.

I was a bright child. Nobody else touched sound,
so I shuddered away from the raised dots
that captured my name. Braille cells.

At playtime I was an empty space
among footballs. I stayed bilingual
for only minutes, afraid to be trapped

in a lonely alphabet.
Now silence arrives, enveloped. The dense paper
spins in my hands. Is it upside down?

Is this the love poem in which I'm a cobra?
My thoughts have arrived in the post.
I guess I'm somewhere, embossed.

On Her Partial Blindness

When I consider how to represent
my sixth of working light, my words collide
with your fear of death. Your visions hide
the blindness born with me. You mourned sight sent
before you into death. Let me invent
a new account – half-light to place beside
your grief – the beauty of blind life denied.
I'd rather exploration than lament:
sight as lost paradise. So my poems need
to make a sense I'm neither banned nor blessed
but breathing here. I want to have my state
revealed as thousands at my bidding read
as I eat, sleep, kiss, swear, get children dressed.
I feel and write. I do not stand and wait.

T
H E
E Y E
C H A R T

I scowl towards his voice. He says the map
marks how far vision goes. If I could creep

up close I'd learn the journey. His technique
restricts me to a chair so he can track

how far I travel down the chart alone
before I pause. I grope in the third line –

my limit the next shape I recognize –
then stop. No way. I still believe my eyes

can hold a solar system, catch all lights,
deliver to the doctor alphabets

as small as atoms. But this world is smudge.
I'm huddled at the bottom of the page,

trying to hide my dark. Wherever I am,
I've bypassed every symbol I can name

and stumble at my vision's borders
where letters are illegible as stars.

The View

Vision is still a draft.
The brain corrects the eye's syntax.

The trees are black lines, their roots seeking nutrients in
    blue earth.
The box on stilts will be a cathedral.

Those holes will become your face.
We walk on our hands over a deep blue ground.

Girl Without a Pearl Earring

She took them off to sleep.
Or did Vermeer insist

she left them in the realm
of oils and spirits?

Though it's the same smell
as my mother's workroom

Vermeer did not paint me.

Please never say to me
woman with disabilities.

They are not jewels.
I cannot put them down.

Functional

In my beginning was a storm
when cerebral palsy formed
a landscape.

Several synapses
broke. My right side's close
to a wilderness,
slashed with dud roads.

The left gets WIFI; the right gets running
ink and cancelled ferries.
I did try to message
my recalcitrant foot while professionals
drew sad blue faces on my soles
but I can't insist
if the infrastructure's
ragged.

The right hand dabbles
in the alphabet and selects
safe surfaces to lean on.
Tradition marked my hands
the deft and the daft
but the right's a reasonable mimic. Vision's
in pieces.
Colour survived. Depth's gone.
Kilometres of optic
nerve are down.
My hearing missed the storm and is briskly
capable of detail. Ovaries busy
in the standard rhythm.
Few prompts reach
the brittle back of my brain.
Towards the front
my Greek verbs pause, surprised.

Diagnoses

Epilepsy wrecks the place then leaves
six scented candles on. Note on the door.
You kept me up all night, you bastards. E.
Cerebral Palsy cries. Dyspraxia
doesn't know how to help and drops a plate.

For all these housemates I am somewhat cramped
although B12-Deficiency's asleep
and Corneal Abrasion is a guest.
Anxiety moved out but left her stuff
while Asthma works elsewhere in summertime
and in midwinter likes the door ajar.

'Who hid my cigarettes? Dyspraxia!'
Cerebral Palsy and Partial Sight block out the noise.
Twelve thousand games ago they bought the house.
Dyspraxia upsets the Scrabble board.
Cerebral Palsy hunts for missing blanks.
BRRRP BRRRRRP BRRRRRRRRRP!
'Hi guys, it's Migraine. Think I lost my key.'

Disabled Person's Travel Card

Council, council, let me on the bus
That you let me on last week.
Oh no, Ms Watt, you can't go on the bus
For we don't know where you live.
So off I went to get proof of address
And I thought I'd sorted out the mess
But the council tore it up.

Council, council let me on the bus
That you let me on last week.
Oh no, Ms Watt, you can't go on the bus
For we need a doctor's note.
So I got them a note to make it clear
That I'm still disabled, like last year.
But the council tore it up.

Council, council, let me on the bus
That you let me on last week.
Oh no, Ms Watt, you can't go on the bus.
We need two sick notes, not one.
The neurologist said *I know you know*
That cerebral palsy won't just go.
Still, here's a form to tell them so.
But the council tore it up.

Council, council, let me on the bus
With my lifelong reasons why.
Oh no, Ms Watt, you can't go on the bus
For your picture isn't straight.
So I sent a note to my MSP
And he wrote a poem in praise of me.
But the council tore it up.

Council, council, let me on the bus
With my lifelong reasons why.
Oh no, Ms Watt, you can't go on the bus
For you're trying to rip us off.
I showed the form to my sister-in-law
And we typed all night till our nerves were raw
But the council tore it up.

Council, council, let me on the bus
With my pile of paperwork.
Oh no, Ms Watt, you can't go on the bus.
We require a note from God.
So I went to church and knelt to pray.
God sent me a letter the very next day.
But the council tore it up.

Council, council, stop. I've had enough.
I've had all that I can stand.
Oh good. Your application went
Exactly as we planned.

Petition

They're making a paper bridge
in the dead centre of Market Street,
using strangers' names as rivets.

Soft-voiced I'm chivvying faces
that scurry past in cagoules
as the rain begins. I envy

the hassle of gulls over my head,
surprised how easy
it is to scare students

who pull their addresses close
like small children,
or who just vanish.

I stay there, nonetheless, knowing
someone who believes in balance will come
striding onto the bridge to add their name.

Ghazal

Free for the first time I adored the dark.
Close to the sea I daundered in the dark.

Seventeen. My short immortal phase.
Was I too young to understand the dark?

A blurred scream at the bottom of my bag –
my rape alarm, which I kept in the dark.

I know your surname now. It's on the news.
Murderers make it hard to love the dark.

You remembered my small daughter's name.
Some acquaintances are in the dark.

My mother lives as though the world's on fire.
I thought that she was wrong about the dark.

I trusted my three streets, the wind,
the sea, a dead cathedral built of dark.

Before I felt that consequences were there
I dared walk-shortening wynds, dark or no dark.

I got to keep my surname off the news
although I hirpled homewards in the dark.

Swallow

Stay very still, or she'll be off again,
I tell myself, as she makes scrambled eggs.
She hasn't eaten all day. *Don't tell Mum,*
she instructs, rolling back a sleeve to show
the dark blue swallow travelling up her arm,
far above vetoes. Of all the shop's spells
for happiness: hearts, dragons, family names,
she chose to be a summer visitor,
born here, but always ready to flit,
the silhouette of good news some of us
are still prepared to look for. The songbird
will help her survive long distance, she says.
Veteran sailors opt to draw its picture
on their chests, after the perfect compass
that spins in its small head, able to guide
them home no matter what. I stroke the charm –
just colour on bare skin. *Of course,* I say,
shaping my palms to make a silent nest.
For weeks afterwards the secret flutters.

Evangelist

Please will you let me pray for your feet?
It's her third request this week.
If I believed, I would demand a warning.
I would ask God to mark this wet-eyed woman
a hazard on my route, like icy steps,
or that North Street blind corner.
Yes I smile. I can make her disappear.
But she stands gawping at my lace-up shoes.
I'm late for lunch, lurch past. *Don't fret.*
I'm off to see a friend, but no one slipped
my happiness onto her mappa mundi.
I prowl on her world's edge like a bad dream.
So now I shut my eyes, letting her shape
a woman she'd prefer out of the air.

Fireblue

Outlineless
I can just sit here
and no one,
no one,
will come looking
for me or for anyone else.

No one will worry
vicariously
because I have gone downstairs
and disenchanted my ankles.

No one will strain
to find my wedding bells
or my dreadful childhood
in which there may have been
too much chintz.

No one will break a mirror
over my browbush,
such as it is.

I can just sit here
outlineless
with a flecked flame.
Grinning.
Fireblue.

Dear Words

Babble to Scrabble to scat –
who makes decisions on that?

Ritual but not lautir.
Habitual but not lautibah.
Which of you are dictionary-proofed?

Why is table sense
but elbat dennuhs?

Babble to Scrabble to scat –
who makes decisions on that?

When did 'bleh' leap into the language?

What can be caught through amniotic fluid?
Dear green phonemes?
Do you know *The Jeely Piece Song* from a Hoover?

Parallel
Parable
Elbarap

What is nonsense? What is not?
What is pure linguistic snot?

Efasnu krad esnesnon?

Esnesnon. Esnesnon.

Did I misspell that right?

Babble to Scrabble to scat –
who makes decisions on that?

Scold's Bridle

This piece of kit seems history's grimace
At a bad joke. A costume built to blur
Woman and demon. Its metal glower
Will hold her still for days to come. Speechless.

Domestic violence. Pride of place. Just try
Gossiping through a kilogram of iron.
Trussed up. Famous as the local siren.
You won't last long. Feel your opinions die,

Your mouth well schooled by cuts and wolf whistles.
They knew how to hit home, the artisans
Who hammered out this lump with calloused hands.
It couldn't happen now, their workshop bustle's

Long gone. We'd never make a gag
So crude. Don't fret. We know so much better.
This curb's superfluous. Want a good fetter?
Then all you need is shame to hold your nag.

She'll never get her tongue over the bit
If you just tell her she invited it.

The Ain Sakhri Lovers

So he made love. He chose that pebble
then chipped away till he felt their double life
moaning beneath his talented fingers.

Now they're cherished, kept in a glass boudoir.
Eleven thousand years of passion
aroused by this pair. The first lust in art.

A fertility prayer? Or a boast
to prove how long he could last? Turn the rock.
Their embrace is the earliest porno.

A stone penis swaggers in your palm.
Then breasts. A vulva. Is this just a scratch
scraped at by testosterone in some cave?

Well, place them right way up, and they look rapt,
stroking each other's pitted pebble skin
as though it's baby-soft. Their hands get everywhere,

exploring this fresh creature they've become.
A couple. It hopes it will be stronger with four lungs,
that through four retinas, life might seem clear.

Pregnant and Squint

I had a holiday from awkwardness. *Can you have sex?* was solved. Most people have been or known a doubled self like us. Briefly my conditions were disabled.

Test to term I never had to console a passer-by spooked by my movement. People knew what to say. *When are you due? Do you know what you're having? Yes, a break.*

We were disconcertingly well. Nothing Abnormal Detected said midwives' scribbles. Just before childbirth, everyone's disabled. For me, same old, same old. I had cohabited with fatigue for years; my balance was dreadful; I already leaked.

Suddenly I had twice the rights on buses. I could be the belly, if I liked, or the girl balanced on a semi-circle. I qualified for both the reserved seats.

I liked the quaint but truthful phrase 'with child'.

The government forced me to list what I couldn't do. I had to excise you from my answers. Whilst I described the most disastrous days, the falls, the fits, the faff, the time I collapsed while trying to use a tampon, my oddly capable body made your kidneys.

Seahorse

As though a seahorse drifted in their ward
The night shift blank your father. He can't be.
Generally, they chase away the fathers

But my cerebral palsy holds him here.
Until we are discharged they'll have to bear
The strangeness of a man strapped to an infant

And crooning Louis Armstrong whilst I boak.
I am mostly opioids this evening,
But every single question comes to me.

You still need to be stowed on somebody
and I'm admonished not to carry you
so your father must be like a seahorse.

Infant Feeding Cup with Painted Turtle

Late Middle Kingdom
Ca. 1850-1700 BCE

I wish I'd had the comfort of this cup
when I was wishing my daughter back inside me,
safely on the foetal monitor,
nourished by a competent placenta –

crying, because how *did* we evolve?

Four thousand years. Still turquoise.

Goodness knows how the glaze is still in place.

I'd have tucked it in my bag with nipple shields,
if I'd known breastfeeding can be brittle –

If I'd known to expect the double pump,
the too-brusque midwives who took my child away

and fed her my colostrum at their desk.

You can't cup feed. You've not been on a course.
Neither had whoever used this cup.

Terror came in with the too slow, too sparse milk.
Percentages of lost weight felt like curses.

Turtle, why are you charged
with the magical management of newborns?

Why are you marked on a tool
for a breastfeeding crisis, when you hazard

your own infants to the sand?

My Baby Belongs to the Health Board

My baby belongs to the Health Board.
I feel like we've got her on loan.
And parents are here by permission
In this baby-processing zone.

They schedule perpetual visits
and set an intractable sum.
I am the square root of my baby.
I do have a name, besides Mum.

They draw me a breastfeeding table.
I don't know what that's all about:
headwords and columns and so on.
Milk in and then excrement out.

I'm wrecked and depressed and exhausted
and motherhood is an exam.
I stare at the scales as my daughter
first gains and then loses a gram.

I'm only confused by these pamphlets.
'cause none of the diagrams match.
With what magic formula does one
correct a sub-optimal latch?

It might be a bit sore at first, dear,
before it becomes a routine.
There's bruises on my areolae.
What level of sore does she mean?

My baby belongs to the Health Board.
She fell off a centile today.
Forgive me my postnatal terror;
I'm worried they'll take her away.

West Scotland Area Quaker Meeting

The roof will not do. The house will not do. It isn't paradise. And of course, we want to move to heaven – somewhere airy, circular and new.

Hence the dissonance of fixing what to do about the roof. It's unfashionable to say *But I love it here. It's beautiful. Just don't touch the speckled wall with the asbestos.*

Like an unwontedly gentle doorkeeper the roof lets in the rain. All the rain. Always. In a city whose reputation is sopping wet. I weave between buckets on my way to peace.

I live in the religion, not the house, although I miss the library's blue swirls. When Covid closes the house, we go through a blue hyperlink to God, or whatever spiritual shorthand suits. Silence spreads through all the west coast islands.

Machiavelli's Baby

Oh look. Here are my feet. Wow!

Beware the sleekit neonate.
Wise parents will not hesitate
to introduce a strict regime
that tells their daughter when to dream.

HELP!!!!!!!! Where did you go?

The cot's a moral training zone:
that child must learn to sleep alone.
Don't pick her up or she'll expect
the adult world to genuflect.

Daddy made a noise!

Appropriate maternal choices
restrain an avarice for voices.
Try not to answer every cry:
she'll waste your mornings on the sly.

Yay! Person!

The supervillain in the sling
coerces you to walk and sing.
Job done, the screaming disappears.
She's got you sussed. Those aren't real tears.

Doze, breast, play, doze, breast, play...
Bored now.
I wonder what the loudest noise I can make is....

A-ee-gah-gah-gah-ee-oo

Guess what? We have a plan for you.
Wow! Here's your magic jiggle chair!

Let's strap you in and leave you there.

NO!

We settle you with ogre tales
and then conspire to cut your nails.
While such skulduggery's afoot
you dream-nurse in your blue-flowered suit.

Why Am I Not Like a Swift?

Dear lord and father of birds
did you never think
how it might ease the terrifying nights with a newborn –

when I think I might drop or vomit on my daughter
because I moved my head –

if we had brains like those of swifts or swallows –
one hemisphere asleep,
the other active?

Suppose our shattered halves could take shift
and shift about
like addled parents?

I covet asymmetric slow wave sleep
and you won't give it,
god.

I can't leave my new daughter in a mud cup or a crevice.
Colic insists I hold and sing to her
though only my breasts are awake.

Alone in the spinning night I briefly hate her father
who is finally asleep beside us.

Immortal invisible
                    what were you thinking?

To keep me awake
                    to keep her alive

the singing is a safety protocol.

Mother

Consider now the figures on the glass.
They change no nappies, neither do they nurse,
Seated in their iridescent idyll.
I nurse my daughter high on a dour blue
Wooden bench. I am a novice mother
Awkwardly surmising how breasts work.

We have gone back to my sporadic work
to hear a lecture. I prefer the glass.
One of those blue blobs must be a mother.
The church sends words to sleep. My colleagues nurse
Strong questions. Swaddled in dark blue
We nod off, drifting in the kirk's cold idyll.

As a mother must I build an idyll?
A colleague asks am I doing any work?
Soon I'll teach my daughter words for blue.
The days seem hazardous as scattered glass.
It seems as though my sole work is to nurse
Through this first semester as a mother.

Perhaps I am too tired to be a mother.
Life as a streak of blue could be an idyll.
But if I were a colour who would nurse
My newborn, whose survival is my work?
The university can mother glass,
Cosseting colour, nourishing the blue.

Still, a small child needs more care than blue
So, for now, I'm first and foremost mother.
Christ's mother must be somewhere on the glass.
Maybe her lactation was an idyll.
If the messiah realised how breasts work,
No lessons from a blue and hurried nurse.

Perhaps it was a rigmarole to nurse
God the squiggle/spiral/dash of blue
As though the artisans who did this work
Had never thoroughly observed a mother.
Bleeding nipples may distort an idyll.
His mother winces on the chapel glass.

The constant work of a new nursing mother
May with time transform into an idyll.
God has clamped down on her blue glass nipple.

Child and Shadow

Last year you were an extension of my shadow.
Now you birth your own bouncing shadow
bound to you by early morning lamplight.
This is my second birthday as your mother.
Your offspring gallivants across the wall.

Obol

You blank the sanctioned surfaces of toys –
soft, squishy, made deliberately safe –
in favour of torn paper or cat fluff,
food wrappers, whoknowswhats and houseless keys.
You bounce towards our corner chaoses,
ensconced for many years. I babyproof
wild floors as best I can, but stuff, stuff, stuff,
slow shoddy reflexes, haphazard eyes.
It's half my life since I felt this disabled.
What if I miss ten pence? The small change locks
your windpipe. You go flop. You travel care
of Charon, the ethereal curmudgeon.
My partial sight sends you across the Styx
and as your mother I have paid your fare.

Hoard

Because our daughter might be knocked unconscious by falling godknowswhat; because the room, a shrine to cardboard, is a shrine to fire – how does a child grow safely in a hoard? Fire and Rescue say she cannot stay here. Ten days to lose the hoard and keep the child. We must make a fit space for a child from this, the flat's subconscious. Daleks live here like malevolent bins. Pregnant boxes, ancient chairs. By Tuesday I would pay to have a fire eviscerate the hoard. Please help us, fire.

Take everything away, except our child. When did I start to creep around the hoard? When did I become so junk-unconscious, accepting that the hoard must have its room so we must compress ourselves to live here? Porcelain has more rights than people here and so does plastic. We christened this guilt the universe room five years ago before we had a child. I wish this were a dream-drill: my subconscious preparing for disaster. *If the hoard retains its rights this happens. Shift the hoard.* But no, the ultimatum is still here. Social Work are not from my subconscious.

Our life proves flammable. Instead of fire we inch towards clear floor space for our child. This week's a prayer to binbags for a room that she can move in, where there is no room for fire or social work. And may the hoard learn to move carefully around the child or go. I want no pregnant boxes here. I wish that I could dissipate the fire laughing/crackling at the edge of my subconscious. The hoard is singing to the fire *Come here.*

Our daughter helps to decorate her room.

Dear Earth

Thank you. I am noticing you more now that there is nothing else to do, nowhere else to go but grass next to motorways. I saw your speedwell and forget-me-nots today, after decades of knowing their names without their faces.

On our licensed walk we found dandelions – *dents des lions* – lions' teeth in a different human language. We blew seeds. My daughter is two but looked nonagenarian – silver fluff in May-lightened hair, the wild hedgerow hair of two months' isolation.

She has begun to ask about germs and play Dodge-the-human. Yesterday she shouted *We are safe*. Perhaps you can soothe the pandemic and we can prune the precautions before they begin to twine around her.

If not I would like my daughter to be like a dandelion – yellow bad-asses that go everywhere because then she would be brief but safe. I wonder if you could arrange this for me?

She would need to shrink until she was minuscule, as light as when she was a zygote, so she could join seeds meandering over your surface. I hope you can consider this proposal.

Sincerely, Nuala

Blue Glass Fish

I know what music is.

I am larger than the foal beside me, but I gather we are not to scale. The foal is a little sad, because she will never have a grown-up tail and she would like to walk, canter or gallop. She is stuck in trot. I need a hand to move me.

I lay in a drawer as dark as the deep sea in case I shattered. Now the human risks me on the shelf. In the drawer I forgot my colours.

Am I for the river or the sea? The books I lean against cannot explain. I was not given gills. There is a tiny crack behind my eye. Perhaps it was deliberate – I don't know. I understand I travelled from a war zone.

The foal is so afraid. I want to ask – who sculpted a flight animal from glass? Horses fear mirrors. They have a long ancestral list of fears. I know that now. I do my best. I wish she had a mare. And a herd bigger than me.

I cool the human's face, am calmest when light jinks through me. Yesterday I learnt 'glass' is a verb. I could be a weapon, if I had to.

Tantrum Villanelle

I brought your boots for quickness, so you seethe.
But I'm so sad that I can't do it yet.
Your self's a tiny room you cannot leave,

And now we are all listening to you grieve.
Your words or size or knowledge will not let
you set the rules, though you are free to seethe.

Due to an obstacle you cannot heave,
a fact, a flaw in this world's etiquette
your self's a tiny room you cannot leave.

I'm sorry that I never thought to grieve
for all the dinosaurs you haven't met.
Somehow or other I forgot to seethe.

There's only so long we're allowed to breathe,
so maybe it is sane to scream and seethe
and be so sad that you can't fly as yet,
wedged tight inside a body you can't leave.

giving up milk

all your life we had been linked devices –

till my pragmatic body switched off milk –

for the last

few months a slowing

concern.

one day your jaw forgot the skill of shifting milk.

working towards this loss

i tried to brace you.

it feels perverse

after thrawn years of cherishing supply.

i couldn't carry you

in case we fell i couldn't hold a bottle.

i made milk.

i woke

breast pumps in desolate

hotels so that my body

wouldn't feel

your absence.

over four years, milk moved   from mystery   to panacea.

breasts turned purposeful   not ornamental.

although your jaw's   forgotten

you have not.

bereaved, you sleep   insistently against me.

Sonnet for a Second Child

Your sister is the person in the air
who has a whole wide life. Away you go.
I was expecting you, but now I know
the scope of infancy and I don't dare.
My love, I have no motherhood to spare.
My body misses milk and wants to stow
another child inside itself, but so?
I choose my settled child. This *is* your share.
Believe me – I would love to know and hold
you in the flesh but we will stay apart.
Your dad and I can kettle sperm, track days.
Listen, my love – I'm on the edge of old.
So no blue plus-signs. Go away, dear heart.
I hope this painful pestering's a phase.

You and I Go Shopping

It's the first time
since you left my body
that we have gone

anywhere
alone.

Being responsible meant being surrounded
by other reflexes and other eyes.

But you are five now, old enough
to walk as instructed,

and I promised you an Easter egg.

Going to the shop is the whole
plot of the morning

although, in all the books you can recite,
no parent moves like me.

Living in my own gait, I forgot
how far I can tilt while clasping
your terrifying lightness.

You promised not
to run,
jump,
jink
or vanish.

Stay safe in your own gait.

Please don't hold my hand.

the disabled

as if we could
all occupy
one phrase

Crip Poetics

'Crip' is in the process of being reclaimed by the disability community' —Wikipedia 2021

But it's just one vowel away from *crap.*
Cripple is not a word I want to darn.
Skilled as we are I doubt that we can turn
a slur out trim and trig as the team strip.
Some words can be reworked, but *crip?* Why drape
ourselves in uselessness? Some words are worn,
like a stained dress. Old sweat won't leave the yarn,
patch as we may. Can one word suit a group?
Like a remoulded but still chafing splint
cripple's done too much harm. Whichever slight
I take in or let out makes someone flinch –
even plain old *disabled.* I had *squint*
made over to mean me, as is my right.
There's no shared word for this that doesn't pinch.

Skivers' Song

Here comes the skivers' song, again.
The tune's a long-lived so and so.
it travels fast from brain to brain

and sets a story on the go:
the quasi-sick. Day in, day out.
The rhetoric clings like mistletoe:

alm-swallower and layabout.
On it drones, won't leave us be.
It's long on hearsay, short on doubt.

One chord for a polyphony
of beings, past and present tense.
Afraid to lose their leper's fee

and stunned by Christ's malevolence
suave beggars dash away from health –
the restoration of a sense –

in case work interferes with wealth.
The figures flee. Their ailment's brief.
They force on me a shadow self

I do not want. I'm not a thief.
Like them I'm squint (my private word)
and still I live with this belief.

So while these ghosts are disinterred,
dissected, glossed, as light relief
once more the song is overheard

on last night's bus. She's lost the source,
but she is quick. "Not you, of course".
It's older than the begging bowl –

almost as difficult to thole.
Strong. Harder to withstand than pain,
here comes the skivers' song, again.

Dialogue on the Dark

and could be the freedom of shapes from their
    cumbersome names.

Allow me my vision at ease.

Eye quietness.

Grievously metaphored sign of a slandered season;
all-purpose hex; assassin; foxes' time.
I wish I could appoint a lawyer for winter.

Let there be an amnesty. Sit. Watch deep blues approach.
Walk. Loiter in low light as though your family were
    blackened trees.

Sounds

I once heard a river as a car,
hovered on a kerb to let the breeze pass.

Traffic is each walker's indrawn breath.
Cyclists make the darkness move nonstop.

I walk on my ears,
the road changing shape as I eavesdrop.

The Pictures

Hear the cinema as a poem.
Try to gather subtitles – white clues
scattered on a white table. Half a phrase –
a mystery between lovers
their disagreement a shower of sparks.

Winter 2020–21

But the blue has morphed since illness
spread out of it, cooried in soon-to-be

corpses and warping my expectations
of the year. Since I wobble,

can't dodge thoughtless strangers,
and rely on wood, on stone, on shopfronts,

I can't walk alone. If the future tense
is here at all it's questions.

When will I go out by myself?
When can I swim?

I watch winter flu and Covid fuck like feral
dogs. I miss winter's moderate

nuisances: slate-chucking storms;
a spell of ice arrest I can accept

since winter gives me
glorious dusk blues.

Frogs

Cycling home through a dawn
migration of frogs,
you edited the war for us
till it was nearly gentle,

although you lost
your proper given name
to all the other Catherines
and were miserably Kay

forever. You hid a fox
in a woodshed, torn to bits
for obstructing the hunt.
You left screaming pilots

out of what we heard.
By now you'd be almost as old
as it's possible to be. I'm glad
you missed this nonsense.

But tell me what to do
when I wake, and I wake
and I wake, and it's still true.

Important Information Enclosed

We're ready to help get your bills down.
We're ready to break down your door
And gift you a pre-payment meter
To stop you from shivering more.

Perhaps you did not learn to budget,
But we can assist you with that.
And can we suggest, in the meantime,
You stay in one room in your flat?

We see you've restarted your asthma.
There's not enough gas for a bath.
You cough when you go to the bathroom.
A more parsimonious path

Could help you to quash all these problems.
And follow our energy plan.
We do understand, and we promise
To help you as much as we can.

Perhaps you could turn down your boiler.
Is your jacket too thin? Buy a spare.
The weather created this crisis.
We want you to know that we care.

The Department of Work and Pensions Assesses a Jade Fish

Once, I held three thousand pale green years.

Should I compare myself to the jade fish?

I am in a museum of difficulties.
I feature in a national catalogue.
Handled, but not with care.

Juliet. Echo.
One. Five. Zero.
Treble Two.
C. That's me.

I'm a fraudster who walks.

Tick this box. Tick this box. Tick this box. Now.

How often do you lose consciousness?
Exactly how much of your life is a mess?

Can you make a cup of tea?

We cannot pay you.

The law says. The law says. The law says.
The phone squanders an hour.
This is because you have as much or more. ....

By the power of brown envelopes
I miss my class on poetics:
'Imagine The Voices of Things'.

Delusions as to Silver

Handwritten sources make it hard to pry.
Asylum records swivel: shit to silver.

Here's when you were admitted, some of why:
The patient has delusions as to silver.

I liked the page illegible so I
could say I worked without disturbing silver.

Bodily health indifferent. Mind awry.
Certain that your hand was spurting silver.

Although my notes are pulped, my sessions by,
still, I also had a phase of silver.

I saw my notes and blanched. I would be shy
if all the future saw of me was silver.

No privacy in archives. Once you die
no protocol can ever staunch the silver.

Does poetry excuse me as a spy
if all it ever shows of you is silver?

A Prayer to Be Released from Prayers

A regular hazard –
as she prays for my feet
my body turns to gospel.

A scrawled-on-skin.
Translated.
Bible-frail.

Rice paper,
my soul folds
in on itself.

I'm sharing a verse
with a man sick
of the palsy.

I ask to be healed
of these moments
that cripple the morning.

Please God, show me my hands,
the early scar,
the necessary bones,

how to take up a life and walk away.

Acknowledgements

Acknowledgements are due to the editors of the following publications. *Atrium, Bad Lilies, Cadenza, The Dark Horse, Gutter, Ink, Sweat and Tears, Magma, Wordgathering.*

Anthologies include *A Year of Scottish Poems* (Pan Macmillan 2018), *The Caught Habits of Language: An Entertainment for W.S. Graham for Him Having Reached 100* (Donut Press 2018), *Stairs and Whispers: D/Deaf and Disabled Writers Write Back* (Nine Arches 2017), *Tools of the Trade: Poems for New Doctors* (Polygon, 2019).

'Delusions as to Silver' was commissioned for the 'Writing the Asylum' project in 2023.

'Important Information Enclosed' was published in the Poetry Archive Now 2023.

I would like to thank the following people: Sandra Alland, Rachael Boast, Khairani Barokka, Gerry Cambridge, Jim Carruth, Katy Evans-Bush, Kathryn Gray, Alyson Hallett, Helen Ivory, Kathleen Jamie, Liz Lochhead, Gillean MacDougall, Rob A. Mackenzie, Helena Nelson, Jeffrey Robinson, the Scottish Poetry Library, Daniel Sluman, Samuel Tongue, Colin Will and the members of Caledonian Poets. Thanks are also due to my parents and to Alastair and Isabelle.

Nuala Watt is a disability activist and Quaker. She has taught English Literature at the University of Glasgow. Her poems have appeared on BBC Radio and in magazines including *Bad Lilies, Ink, Sweat and Tears,* and *Wordgathering.* She views poetry as a form of activism and a method of thinking. *The Department of Work and Pensions Assesses a Jade Fish* is her first full collection.